IT AIN'T ALL ROCKET SCIENCE

3 Success Steps To
Corporate Contracts for
Minority Business Owners

Copyright

Copyright 2018 Dobbins International, Inc. All rights reserved. No part of this book can be reproduced in any form without the written permission of the author and its publisher.

Acknowledgements

This book would not be possible without the love, help and support of so many wonderful and inspiring people. In no specific order I would like to thank Jim Neikirk, Bill Davidson and Art Hersberger, three bosses that pushed, demanded, encouraged and supported me at being my very best, at all times.

Many thanks to Russ Lambert and Cynthia Curry, my brother and sister in Christ that took the leap of faith, wrote books of their own, and through their selfless efforts, gave me courage to write this book.

To Annie Lidge, Shon Raglin, Angela Freeman and Dick Huebner, I owe an unrepayable debt of gratitude for your unwavering support in getting this material in the hands of deserving minority business owners and for your insistence that I see through to completion this effort to reach as many business owners as possible. You truly are the wind beneath these sails.

Jennifer Kem, I stand in my brand voice, being my true authentic self, confidently exhibiting servant leadership from learning and watching you do the same. Thank you!

To Kathy Kidd and Amber Petersen, you made simple and easy the process of getting this book published and into the hands of those that need it most. Your support has been invaluable in my taking the action to "get 'er done!".

A very special thanks to my editors Julie Hiner, Debbie Burns, Flora Moragne and Lynne Hurdle-Price for your truly priceless input and contributions. You guys rock!

Thanks as well to a loving, supporting and encouraging family, know that we are just getting started.

Most importantly, thanks to Our Heavenly Father without whom none of this would be possible. Your Grace and Mercy is sufficient.

Table of Contents

Chapter 1 The Big Money is in Corporate Contracting....................1

Chapter 2 The Challenge for Minority and/or Women Owned Businesses......................................6

Chapter 3 Times Have Changed ...10

Chapter 4 Mindset for Success.....14

Chapter 5 The Struggle is Real.....31

Chapter 6 The Secrets Revealed ..36

Chapter 7 Step #1 – Clarify Your Unclear Value Proposition............37

Chapter 8 Step #2 – Match Your Product / Service Offerings to the Customer's Needs 50

Chapter 9 Step #3 – Make Sure You Are Contract Ready 65

Conclusion...................................76

Next Steps and Additional Resources 79

About The Author 81

Chapter 1
The Big Money is in Corporate Contracting

You dared to start a business and now you hope that your creation makes a difference. And that that difference can stand the test of time. Because what you really want is to build a legacy—something you can hand down to future generations. That is your definition of success, right? Making a difference in not only your lifetime, but over a number of life times.

Wow, what a contribution.

The best and most enduring method for doing this is to make sure that your business has corporate clients.

Corporations committed to buying your products/services allow you the ability to sustain your business over periods of years and decades. And the procedures corporations use to make the purchase decision guarantees this sustainability. There are companies that have been around for over 100 years. Some of them still buy from their original suppliers.

The corporate contracting market is huge. The companies included in the 2017 Global Fortune 500 alone had sales of about $27 Trillion, with the 2017 US Fortune 500 accounting for about $14 Trillion of that. The difference between which companies are included in the global companies and US based companies is based on their headquarters. Knowing the country of origin for these companies is invaluable in understanding current priorities and culture. Volkswagen and BP are included on the Global list. Walmart and Exxon/Mobil are included in both. Imagine if your company could get just one percent of that spend. What would it do to your business? What kind of difference would it make in your life; in the life of your family; in your community and the causes you hold dear?

These companies spend money on most everything.

You name it, they buy it.

Office supplies? Yes.
Staffing services? Yes.
Janitorial services and supplies? Yes.
Computers? Yes.
Cars? Yes.
Technology? Yes.
Consulting work? Yes.
Health and wellness services/products? Yes.

Pick pretty much anything that you can think of and at some point or another a large corporation has bought it; travel, entertainment, food, you name it, they buy it, they buy it all.

The question is never do they buy what you sell, the question is which of the companies is the best fit for the products you sell.

Chapter 2
The Challenge for Minority and/or Women Owned Businesses

While the big money is in corporate contracting, the big problem is that minority business owners and women business owners have been left out. We either were not encouraged to start businesses or were excluded from getting the really big corporate contracts.

Many of us have been in the corporate contracting wilderness for years. We fight and scratch for every little opportunity. We attend countless meetings, expos, conferences and networking events.

We submit proposal after proposal with limited to no success. We are invited to token meetings where within 5-10 minutes we know they aren't serious about doing business with us or letting us proceed to the next level.

We have input our company names and information into countless supplier databases. We have heard over and over and over again, "I will get back to you" or "I will keep you in mind if an opportunity arises".

We don't want to feel like we are not getting opportunities because we are a minority, or because we are a woman or because we are not straight white males. However, we are overcome with the inescapable visual evidence that straight white males seem to not just be getting in, but getting and keeping the bigger contracts.

What is the deal here? Do they golf together? Is it a good old boys network? Do they go to ball games together? Do they attend the same church? Country Club? Do their kids and wives spend all the time together? Is it even possible for my company to just get in the door?

Even those of us that have made it in seem to still be fighting for the crumbs. We always seem to be looking through the glass ceiling and feeling left out from the really big contracts.

We often are left wondering – "is it me?"

That is until now.

Chapter 3
Times Have Changed

Big corporations now understand that those companies with the most diverse employees and the most diverse suppliers have better outcomes. They make more money. Their products and services are attractive to more customers. Their profits (and earnings) increase.

Big companies are actively looking for minority and women-owned businesses to do business with. They have dedicated organizations and team members looking for diverse suppliers across the globe. They even have member organizations like the Billion Dollar Roundtable (BDR) where they share thoughts and ideas on how to drive more opportunity to diverse-owned businesses.

The Billion Dollar Roundtable is a member organization of companies that individually spend over a billion a year with minority and women owned businesses.

The issue today therefore is not: are companies awarding substantial contracts to minority and women-owned businesses—we know from the BDR that billions are spent annually with companies owned by people that look like us. The issue therefore is: are they writing these contracts with *your* company?

As a matter of fact, corporations via the BDR and other similar organizations have yet to reach their target spend levels. They have missions to attract even more diverse-owned businesses for these opportunities.

And *you* can take advantage of this amazing time in the market place with the right blueprint.

It turns out that there is no grand conspiracy to keep specific groups of business owners from these opportunities. This may have been true in the past but not so much today.

The reality is that only a handful of companies have been successful with these opportunities. Until now.

Because now and in the foreseeable future, your company has one of the best opportunities to grow your business to unimaginable heights.

Chapter 4
Mindset for Success

My company has been providing training to minority and women business owners on how to get the really big contracts with the largest companies in the world. We've been at this for over 12 years now. We have spoken at international conferences and have been sought after by major corporations to provide this training - in some cases to provide the training to their procurement staff. We've had clients make minor changes to their businesses and start to get contracts they never thought possible. It, however, was not always like this.

You see, although I had a highly successful career as a supply chain manager for Shell Oil Company (I was even a designated Minority/Women Business Enterprise Coordinator who picked which of the companies, like yours, I would give contracts to as a Shell Buyer). Although I had a highly successful career as a National Accounts Sales Manager for WESCO Distribution, and although I had an amazing professional career, I too struggled when I started my business.

I figured going after contracts with the Fortune 500 would be doable with my background. I've written contracts of over $150M a year for five years or $0.75B. I knew there would be bumps in the road along the way but I made the same mistake most diverse business owners make.

May I share a story with you?

Some 15 years ago I was sitting in a meeting—one of those supplier development council meetings that we are encouraged to participate in for the purpose of meeting corporate representatives. I joined the council, made it to all the mixers, meetings and regular events trying to be seen and get the word out on who we are and what we offer. I had even gotten a committee assignment.

This particular committee was the Strategic Teaming Alliance Committee, which focused on helping minority business owners learn about strategic alliances. Strategic alliances are clearly in my wheelhouse since I have written best in class strategic alliance agreements as a Shell buyer and as WESCO National Accounts Manager. I just knew this was where I was supposed to be.

My participation on this committee would put my company in the best light (I thought), and we would finally get a big contract.

But something that changed my life happened during one of the meetings. It rocked my world. I'd asked the committee chair, a supplier diversity manager for a big oil company, if I could meet with her about doing business with her company.

She leaned over to me and said, "Randall, if you're honest with yourself, you'll realize you're not big enough to do business with us."

That hurt. That hurt! I'm saying to myself "what do you mean I'm not ready to do business with you?" I was so confused. I kept thinking to myself "what do you mean I'm not big enough to do business with you? What do you mean I'm not ready? What do you mean, wait your turn?

Wait your turn? What do you mean by all of these other things that go with that?"

And so I was pretty angry about it. I was fired up. I went home that night and I'm like, you know, how dare somebody tell me I'm not ready—again. How dare they tell me I'm not big enough. All of these things went through my head.

And so I decided, I'm not going to accept that as an answer. I'm not going to use that as an excuse. I'm not going to play victim.

Let me figure out what she's really telling me and let me figure out if I can solve the real underlying problem.

Having calmed down, I discovered that what she was really telling me was I had not demonstrated to her what she needed to see. She was letting me know that she had not seen enough to be my advocate within her company. She had not seen the bare minimum she needed to even take the risk and introduce me within her organization.

Wow, how could I have failed to give an advocate the tools she needed to help me?

Once I figured that out, it was like, "oh, OK, OK, that's a problem I can solve."

To solve this, I had to think back to my career as a buyer and as a national accounts manager. I had to really analyze the success traits of suppliers to whom I awarded contracts. What did they do that made me comfortable with their ability to perform? I also had to think through, having gone from field buying to head office buying, what made for a successful supplier, not only for a single location but across multiple regions such as North America. I then had to think through why we as a distributor were highly successful selling into the Fortune 100, an even smaller group of the Fortune 500. What was it about our pitch that resonated with them?

That's when it hit me. It wasn't that I was too small, it was that I did not make clear how I would successfully handle her business. I came off as the corner lot, used car business owner when she was accustomed to dealing with car makers.

Now that I understood the mistakes I was making, it made sense to me why the supplier development manager told me I wasn't big enough. I also then realized that pitching, pitching, pitching without addressing my ability to perform (otherwise known as "capacity") and hoping that perseverance alone would win the contract would most likely cause me to run out of money. If I truly wanted to be successful, I needed to make some changes now!

You may have been in this place where you keep pitching, pitching, pitching, pitching, and hoping that someone recognizes the value that you offer. But I'm here to tell you they won't recognize your value unless you *show* them. And this includes making clear that you can handle the business. A good buyer will never award a contract and hope for the best. It is their job to make sure that every supplier getting a contract can successfully do the job.

When that supplier diversity manager started telling me I wasn't big enough, I was like, "Oh, you're telling me something different".

You're saying that I'm not representing to you that I have either the balance sheet or the capacity to fulfill the requirements that your company has for the products I'm selling. I get it now. There's more than one way that I can solve that problem.

That's when we came up with what we call the Business Partner Blueprint. It solves this very issue.

And we've successfully rolled it out to the tune of millions of dollars for our business. We have also successfully trained thousands of companies and clients over the past 10 years that are really and truly knocking it out of the park with corporate clients. And we are going to share with you what you don't know about the decision-making process and how it affects the way you're perceived by companies. Once you understand this, then you can start putting together a solution that actually becomes compelling and something that they're going to say "Yes, yes, yes. You get me. You understand my business as a buyer. You're who I want on my team."

It is interesting talking to business owners and learning a bit more about why they went into business in the first place. Many say, "I have a heart-based mission. I want to make a difference. I want to be the first in my family. I want to do something that no one in my family's done before. I'm going to do something that people in my community haven't done before. I want to do something that I've seen other people do and I just need to know personally that I can do this and the difference it's going to make for me, for my family, my community. That's why I'm here."

Now let me share something with you. Selling to corporates is a lot easier than selling to anyone else if you do it right. Because we're talking about the really big contracts, a hundred thousand a year, a million a year, 10 million a year, a hundred million a year. All of these are perfectly doable contracts, when you're dealing with corporates and you have the solutions that they're looking for.

You may already have a multi-million dollar business. You know how to get in and pitch but you still aren't breaking through to the really large opportunities. So in this case it really and truly is just a matter of understanding what you need to do to go in and get to the next level. Let's recap and talk about this market. This is a $27 Trillion market with the Fortune 500 alone. Imagine what you could do with one percent of that, or one-tenth of a percent of that.

That's huge.

Think about what it would do for your business if you had one contract for $100,000, a Million, $10 Million. Think about how you can leverage that into bigger and greater opportunities and how that sets you up for the long term success and, dare I say it, *legacy* that you actually hope to create.

Talk about changing your life and your family's life! Think about the education for your kids, getting mom and dad the new house or a bigger house for them to come live with you. Just a whole host of things that you thought you'd be able to do once you got your business to the level of success you wanted. Think about what that first major contract would do for you, and then if you had the skill and the talent to repeat that one-after-the-other because you had a formula that worked well?

It doesn't matter if you haven't made the decision yet as to whether or not corporate contracting is the market you want to pursue. It doesn't matter if you've been struggling to get your foot in the door. It doesn't matter if you got your foot in the door, but you haven't quite figured out how to get around and you don't seem to be getting the opportunities. It doesn't matter if you've been at this for a while. You've been contracting with large corporations, but you've hit the supplier "glass ceiling" where you don't seem to be able to get into the board room for the bigger opportunities.

We're going to address this with your Business Partner Blueprint.

Chapter 5
The Struggle is Real

It was unfortunate that it took me so long to figure this out. I spent sleepless nights trying to figure out how to make the business successful. I had a second job. I was counting pennies like there was no tomorrow—hoping I had money to pay for all the meetings, conferences, gas and yes, sometimes pay for parking. I can't tell you how many times I drove around the block looking for street parking as it was cheaper than paying the hourly rate at the parking lots. I've even had to leave meetings to put money in parking meters. Having cash flow for payroll, let alone having money left over was clearly a challenge. I recall the many direction changes we made as a team. It was one of those "let's just throw it against the wall and see what sticks" strategies. We knew we had a good offering, we just needed to find someone willing to take a chance on us. "Perseverance!"

Back at home, my wife was getting really frustrated. The strain on the relationship was bad. She was holding down the finances for the house. She looked at me one day and asked when was I going to give up on this "business thing" and get a "real" job. She stressed with emphasis that she was getting tired and she didn't see any evidence of things turning around. The solution to this problem, in her mind, was very clear.

Talk about a gut check! I had to decide then and there do I give up on my dream or do I make this work?

If only I had been told "you aren't big enough" sooner, I believe my family would still be intact. I easily could have started writing really big contracts 18-24 months earlier (because I know the elements of the Business Partner Blueprint and I know beyond a doubt that they work). I could have avoided the financial stress at home and at work. I most likely would have had less doctor's visits. I clearly would have been in a better mood during time with the family, I could have had quality vacations and generally a more positive frame of mind as the stress of the business would have been positive.

I could have done a lot of things. I didn't have to let it get this bad. I didn't need to put this much strain on my family and my health. But I just didn't know how to fix it. With this book, you do. So don't let another day go by without a proven plan to land the big contracts you deserve.

Let's talk about your Business Partner Blueprint. Let's talk about how you break the cycle of doing the same things yet expecting a different result. Let's talk about the 3 things you can do right now that will take your company to amazing business heights and position you to compete with any other company in the market place.

Chapter 6
The Secrets Revealed

The 3 steps you can take right now are simple:

1. Offer a product that your customer says is of value to them.
2. Offer product/services in the way your customer wants to buy them.
3. Do the work to make sure that you are "contract ready" or that you are ready for the opportunity a big company is looking to give you.

Chapter 7
Step #1 – Clarify Your Unclear Value Proposition

Let me share with you what went through my head as a buyer when meeting and working with minority and women business owners.

You're more than likely going after business that I had under contract with your competitor. So, the simple answer is you have to be better than they are. I already have a frame of reference around what it takes to be successful to do this work. I've already developed requirements and issued contracts for the work. Now, some of you may be doing something that hasn't been done before, but these issues still apply because you still have to have the corporate buyer that you're talking to, in this case me, understand why they need to use you.

But bear in mind, if somebody currently has the business, then the issue that you're confronted with when pitching your company to a corporate buyer, when it was me for example is, do I believe you can do the job better than the person who currently has it?

I either do or I don't.

If I do, then it's worth having you come in and we'll talk further. If not, I've got to get out of the conversation as politely, and as quickly as I can.

I discovered this just from having talked to so many business owners like you, from having pitched myself, and the issue really and truly is simply this: "Do I believe you're going to bring value?"

So, you may be asking, what's the significance of this? The significance is, if you don't nail this, you've blocked the opportunity to move forward. You might be able to come back. You can fine-tune your pitch and do a whole host of things and you can probably get a second bite at the apple. The biggest significance however is that you've made yourself not relevant to the person that you're talking with.

Being committed to their job though, they may find some other redeeming thing about your presentation. They may find some other places they think they might be able to do something because they just like you for the strength of your personality, or the general capabilities of your company.

However, you want to always be focused on one specific area where you can help them because that's the easiest thing for them to do. A company that knew what they offered and pitched how they thought they could help me always got my best effort. I either could quickly determine where an opportunity might exist or I could quickly let them know we weren't a good fit. In either case it was good for both companies. For mine, I might have a good supplier. For theirs, they knew whether they were wasting time with me or not. It's easier for a buyer to say, yes, this will work in this area. It takes more effort than they may want to take if they reason that they like you, but then have to determine if/where they can find a place to put you.

The issue now is once you know how your approach to a corporate client could be affecting your business, you know that this mistake is costing you business. How do you fix it, and what is it you're trying to fix?

You're trying to fix the specific issue of an unclear value proposition.

So how do you fix it? You make your value proposition

- relevant,
- quantified, and
- uniquely differentiate yourself.

I'm going to give you an off-the-wall example to illustrate this. Imagine you're in a bar and imagine somebody comes up to you. Let's just say you're a woman. I'm a man and a I walk up to you and I say, "hey, how you doing?"

You say "Great", and then you say to me, "hey, tell me a little bit about yourself."

And I say, "well, hey, I'm a guy and I'm here in this bar."

You look at me. Then you go, "well, hey, it's ladies' night. Seventy percent of the people in here are Guys."

Now I know that's a ridiculous example, but I want you to think about that for a second. More often than not during a networking event, supplier's walk up to somebody in a corporation and the representative asks you, what do you do? You unfortunately don't perceive this as an opportunity to talk about your value; which is what it really is. You perceive it as a simple question. What do you do? You say, I have a staffing company; I have a janitorial company; I have an IT supply company; I have a SharePoint or cloud service company; I have a pipe valves and fittings company. I supply this, that and the other and what not. And so just in that answer, you've not differentiated yourself.

You now, within 5 seconds, have fallen into that 70 percent of the guys that are in the bar that only identified themselves as a "guy".

What's required here is a reframe of the entire interaction. You have to come back and you have to have done your homework about the company you're talking with and you now have to make your response relevant. You have to quantify the value. You have to uniquely differentiate yourself.

Let's just switch it a little bit. Let's say hypothetically you said you were a staffing company after they asked, "what do you do"? Rather than say you're a staffing company, try this.

You say "we are a staffing company that provides _____ type of expertise. Our recruiting process has identified people that are uniquely qualified for these positions. Recent benchmarking indicates that our staff is 15 to 20 percent more productive than our competitors, and we've seen that impact projects on our client's end by coming in about 15 percent faster and about seven to 10 percent under budget". (Big note here: You better be able to provide proof of these numbers through either customer testimonials, case studies, research reports or some other manner. Do not make misrepresentations. Nothing good can come from a misrepresentation!)

There you go. Relevant. Value Quantified. Unique differentiation because you said what it is that your people do that's different relative to the competition.

Before we move on, I can't stress enough how critical it is that your target customer has a crystal clear understanding of your business. So, I want to give you 3 additional thoughts. Working through these will make it easier to accomplish the tasks above. More precisely, they will help you stand out against your competitors.

When seeking a corporate contract, here are 3 additional things you need to be able to present to a decision maker or influencer.

1. The total cost for your business.

You need to be able to project, track and specify the cost from concept creation to point of sale for everything that your business offers.

2. The standard total cost for your industry.

If you can show figures that benchmark what most businesses in your industry put out, it'll show that you're clearly an expert in your market and allows you to position your business as a solid choice.

3. The unique position/results your business provides.

After clearly cementing your expertise, you need to showcase why and how your business is getting a specific result that the corporation is unable to achieve. This shows exactly why they should choose your business.

Take some time now and think about not what you offer, but what benefit a customer gets from your offering.

Think of it this way: A car has a satellite radio in it as an offering. The benefit or value, however, is that you get to listen to your favorite music all the time, everywhere, so that you have the control over the type of mood you want to experience during your driving experience.

As we say in the industry: "Sell the sizzle, not the steak".

Chapter 8
Step #2 – Match Your Product / Service Offerings to the Customer's Needs

Let's talk about product and service fit, the second of the 3 steps you need to get the really big contracts with the largest companies in the world.

This is what I like to call "stop trying to sell tires to a new car shopper."

Let me set this up a little bit. Imagine you're going in to buy a new car. You walk into the showroom, you have a really good idea of what you want to buy. You've already figured out that you're ready to make a pretty substantial investment.

You know what you need the car to do, whether it's a minivan, sports car, two-seater, four door, whatever—you've done all the work.

You know what you want as far as accessories. You might be a little open on color. You might be open on a couple of different things, but you have a really good idea cause you're in the mode to buy a new car. Now imagine you're walking around and you're looking and getting excited because you're seeing one or two or three that you think you really want. Then, this real eager salesperson across the lot sees you.

They're just excited, big smile on their face, all kinds of enthusiasm. You're getting ready to get prepared for the conversation because you are really hoping that they can actually get you across the finish line. You expect them to make a difference based on what you know you need.

Finally, the salesperson says, "hello and how can I help you today?"

And you say, "I'm in the market for a new car. What do you have? What can you do for me?"

And he says, "well, actually today I want to talk to you about buying a set of tires."

And you go, "what? I'm here to buy a new car. Why are you talking to me about a set of tires?"

He goes, "yeah, I know, I know you're here to buy a new car, but you, you're going to need tires and I'm the guy that can get you those tires for that car."

You're going, "no, I don't need tires. I'm shopping for a new car. And besides I'm not going to need tires for another three to four years. And oh by the way, this is the first of a fleet of cars, in which case, whoever it is I buy the car from will be able to handle the tires for me and the maintenance and the oil changes and everything else. So no, I'm really not interested in buying tires."

Once again, another crazy example, kind of like the one we used about the bar, but I'm using it to make a point. And the point is simply this.

A lot of times you go into conversations with a corporate representative and you come across like the tire salesperson. And here's what I mean by that. The largest companies have begun to bundle a lot of products and services and more often than not, you, me, and those like us are only selling one item in the bundle. They're looking to buy a new car, we're selling tires. We may have some of the world's best tires, but the tire is only a small part of what they're looking for.

You've got to stop doing that.

You have to understand how it is your customer goes to market. How do you do that? You discover how they purchase what it is you sell. You can conduct informal research and try to figure out how does Wholefoods, for example, go about selecting their lettuce provider? Do they source it internationally? Do they source it locally? Is it organic? Do they get the lettuce and carrots and tomatoes from the same person or do they just find lettuce farmers? How do they do it? Is there a specific requirement that they have in their lettuce and does it matter whether it's iceberg versus romaine versus whatever else?

How does General Motors, how does Exxon Mobil, how does Coca Cola, how does Dell, how do any of these companies go to market for the products and services you offer.

Pick any company. Think about what it is you sell and find out how it is they go to market.

1) Do they buy what you sell?
2) Do they buy it as a standalone item or do they buy it as a bundle?
3) Next thing, how do they measure performance?

Additionally, you're going to have to be a little bit more creative, you can do some research on their total cost of ownership or how is value measured? Is it purely on price? Is it price and services? Is it cost reduction? Is it a whole host of factors? It is imperative that you figure out how they measure performance and how they measure value.

You might have to see if you can find some friends to help you here. It is likely that you are only one to two degrees of separation on LinkedIn from someone that can help you with the answer to this question.

(And yes, you need to be on LinkedIn to find somebody in that company who knows the person who buys what you're looking for and you can just have a discovery conversation with them.)

Your introduction should be along the lines of, "I'm not calling to sell you something. I'm calling to find out a little bit more about how you go to market on something." There's a good chance they'll take that call and give you some feedback. Or they'll point you to a source where you can get the information. This one might be a little bit of work, but it's very doable.

You can review Wall Street Journal's Today's Top Supply Chain and Logistics News section. It provides best practices and innovations in select industries. This is a great benchmarking source as it provides you with current practices in your industry and what potential customers are seeking.

You can take full advantage of advocacy agencies like the National Minority Supplier Development Council, Women's Business Enterprise National Council, the Hispanic Chamber and a number of others. Their representatives are more than happy to introduce you to a corporate member either via a scheduled meeting or during one of their networking events.

You can talk to your competitors when you're at a mixer, a networking event or any other type of thing where you just kind of find out their experience in a specific market segment, and what are some of the things customers are now asking them to do.

You can attend a networking event or a mixer or something else to talk more with your corporate clients and ask how do they know when they have a good supplier? What are some of the things that the supplier does?

I'll give another example that just recently came up. It's one of the best examples to give you a sense of how the really big companies are viewing their business from an internal perspective.

I was talking to a friend at a large chemical company and they said, "you know Randall, we are at that point right now where we are actually looking for managed print services. When a potential supplier walks up to me and says, 'I own a print shop' I'm like, I can't really do anything with that."

I asked, "what do you mean about managed print services"?

And she said, very simply, she needs to be able to tell her end users that the company has entered into a contractual arrangement where, when the end user pushes a button on their computer:

- that print job is going to show up at whatever international location that company has and
- it's going to include all of the requirements that the company has around our logo and
- the fonts that we use and
- all the myriad of specifications that we use regarding external print work.

She said that if somebody can do that for her so that when her end-user pushes that button, it shows up where she needs it to show up, conforming to corporate standard, then that's her hero.

Now you're about to imagine somebody like Fedex Kinko's or Fedex Office could do that very easily. But no, I don't want you to feel overwhelmed or threatened. I don't want you thinking that you can't compete with this level of service or that there is no way you can do that.

This is the game you're stepping into and yes, you can do it! There's a methodical way to get there quickly and profitably. You've just got to know what the game is. We have said before: "Learning what you don't know allows you to create what you can't yet imagine." That's why learning how big corporate customers go to market is the secret to your business success.

Chapter 9
Step #3 – Make Sure You Are Contract Ready

You *never* want to leave the perception that you're not ready for the business. I'm telling you, point blank, I knew within 10 seconds of a conversation whether or not a company could do business with Shell Oil Company.

It's a bold statement, right? But I want you to think about it. The issue was not could you sell something and could I use it? The issue was, did it make sense for me to bring you in and potentially disrupt my supply chain?

Now, once you understand large corporate structures and how they measure value and how systems and processes work, you never want to disrupt a supply chain unless you're doing something totally disruptive so that you can tear it up to remake it and do it better. That, however, is not what typically happens with a lot of the products that you sell, I sell, and minority business owners sell. Those truly disruptive products and services are handled very differently and will be the subject of another book. What we're talking about are the things that big companies routinely buy; and no company is going to disrupt their process to bring in a new supplier.

They have to find a way to bring it in so that it's not disruptive. That gets you into the whole conversation about whether your company is ready to do business. If you are ready to do business, there's a good chance that what you do is not disruptive. If it is disruptive, then the value or the savings has to outweigh the disruption.

Just some quick math—it costs about three to five percent for a corporation to switch from one supplier to another. The condition for change is around three, four, five percent in savings. If you do the quick math, you need to bring a solution that is somewhere between seven to 10 percent cheaper than what they're currently getting. And that's cheaper total cost and price, so if you're competing on price, be careful.

I will share with you something a friend shared with me: "there's somebody else willing to go out of business faster than you."

Rarely do you want to compete exclusively on price unless it's just one of those markets, one of those commodities, or one of those competitive situations you find yourself in. The caveat here is when you can establish yourself as a subject matter expert or demonstrate domain expertise in how you can offer a lower price. This builds tremendous rapport with your customer. Buyers otherwise assume that you are trying to "buy" the business by offering a lower price and become suspicious of your offer as a result.

You want to compete on value. In order for you to demonstrate that there is 7-10% value, you've got to be able to replace whoever currently has the business. You have to serve all the different locations the company needs for you to provide your products and services. And to do this, you're going to need partners.

The days of doing it by ourselves are long gone. Today, in order for us to deliver the products and services, we have to do things differently. It is too costly to try and build a business that competes with companies 2, 3 or 10 times the size of ours.

However, if we can successfully partner with 2, 3 or 4 other companies and build out a robust product /service offering as well as a deep bench, we now are formidable. This is where you need a Business Partner Blueprint.

This is where you need a solution that allows you to solve:

Problem #1- enhancing your value proposition because you can make a bigger impact

Problem #2 - actually having a product/service bundle that a corporation can look at and fit right into their process with minimum disruption

Problem #3 – knowing that if they give you an order, you can perform. Can you do the work? Can you grow with them and into bigger opportunities as they buy new companies and acquisitions and mergers and other kinds of things?

You can ride shotgun with them and be right there. That's the position you want to be in. That's when you know you're playing at the big table with the big boys, that's it.

That's what it looks like.

It turns out that when you put your Business Partner Blueprint together, you are setting your business up for long term success, not just with the really big companies, but with any customer segment you go after.

We're now in what I refer to as the partner economy. We see it in the tech space. That group will partner with a whole host of other companies. We see more partnering or strategic alliances among and between big corporations. They are going it alone less and less. We actually see high levels of partnering activity among women business owners. Women business owners will partner more than minority business owners.

So, the imperative right now for your business success is to have a Business Partner Blueprint that confidently, boldly and profitably gets you your unfair share of this $27 Trillion market that is looking for people like you and me to come participate in.

The action for you here is simple.

1) Be clear on what it is you do that gives you a unique and distinctive competitive advantage in the marketplace. Guard this closer than Coco-Cola guards their formula.
2) Find out what additional products and services above and beyond those you offer are of value to your target customers.
3) Begin actively seeking out other companies that offer the products / services that are not strategic to your future but are strategic to theirs and begin exploratory conversations.
4) Make sure you do the work to understand your current

cultures and the culture you want to have. Find partners whose cultures complement yours. This way you are building in long-term sustainable success in creating a mutual interdependency that helps make all partners' businesses grow.

Conclusion

There has never been a better time to be in business. The global economy is positioned to grow like it hasn't grown in decades. Big companies are aggressively embracing diversity and inclusion. This focus is extending to the supply base. Big companies are becoming more creative in finding solutions for minority and women business participation. They however will not relax their standards.

Suppliers will have to meet existing requirements to get into the corporate supply chain and take advantage of the opportunities. As a matter of fact, we should expect that competitive pressures to the supply chains of big corporations will actually raise the bar. We therefore need to prepare to compete at an even higher level.

Once we know what's required we can clearly compete, contribute and win—even at the highest levels!

Let me repeat: learning what we don't know about how big companies go to market allows us to create solutions we can't yet imagine.

The first step in this process is to take advantage of the 3 secrets I revealed to landing the really big contracts. We first must have a compelling value proposition that a customer says is meaningful to them. We then have to offer products and services the way our customer wants to buy them, not the way we want to sell them. We finally have to be contract ready. We have to demonstrate that we have the capacity to handle current and future business.

Contracts of this magnitude allow us to build businesses of our dreams; make the contributions to society we hoped; and create legacy for those after us.

"Think Big, Do Big!"

Next Steps and Additional Resources

We welcome the opportunity to discover more about your business and your hopes for a legacy. Please feel free to contact us at one of the following to discover more on our offerings to assist you in developing your dream business:

Minority Business Owners and Women Business Owners:

www.BusinessPartnerBlueprint.com
WeCare@BusinessPartnerBlueprint.com

Corporations:
www.DobbinsInternational.com
Info@DobbinsInternational.com

About The Author

Randall Dobbins is the Founder and Creator of the Business Partner Blueprint. For over 15 years he has trained hundreds of successful diverse companies in the art of landing large corporate contracts. As a buyer, seller, and minority business owner, he has spent years perfecting processes for designing, creating, negotiating, implementing and managing strategic partnerships for the world's largest corporations, including Shell Oil Company, Westinghouse Electric Supply Company, and his own company Dobbins International.

Randall now has created a framework to help disadvantaged business owners (like you) land corporate contracts that can transform your company. Get started today.